DOG TRIVIA

FUN Q & A
FOR DOG LOVERS

Copyright ©Dog Trivia (Fun Q&A For Dog Lovers)
All rights reserved. This book or any portion thereof may not be reproduced or used in any manner whatsoever without the express written permission of the publisher except for the use of brief quotations in a book review.
Printed Worldwide
First Printing, 2019

Introduction

How well do you know your dog? This book is full of fun trivia about dogs. You can either read for fun or quizz your friends or family on how well they know their furry friends.

How to read or play?

Play to win or read for fun, the choice is yours!
To play for fun, all you need to do is read through the questions and see if you know the answers. It can also be great fun to read the questions out to family or friends, and see who knows the most about cats.

If you want to play to win, pick either 10 to 15 questions each. You get 1 point for each correct answer. The winner is the person with the most points.

Where are the answers?

For each set of questions, the answers are located on the reverse of the page. There are two answers per page (1 top and 1 bottom), so try to cover the answers to the questions you have not seen.

Q1. Approximately how many words can a dog learn?

 QUESTIONS

Q2. How many hours do puppies sleep a day on average?

A1. 1000 words

 ANSWERS

A2. 18 to 20 hours

Q3. What is the fastest dog breed?

 QUESTIONS

Q4. What is the dog population of the world?

A3. Greyhound

 ANSWERS

A4. 400 million

Q5. Which is the most popular dog breed for pets?

 ## QUESTIONS

Q6. What is the average lifespan of a dog?

A5. Labrador Retriever

 ANSWERS

A6. 10 to 14 years

Q7. Do smaller breed of dogs live longer or shorter than larger breeds?

 QUESTIONS

Q8. Which US President put in place a dog tax?

A7. Longer

 ANSWERS

A8. Thomas Jefferson

Q9. What is the heaviest dog breed?

 QUESTIONS

Q10. Which dog breed has the shortest height?

A9. Mastiff

 ANSWERS

A10. Chihuahua

Q11. What was the name of the first dog to go to space?

 QUESTIONS

Q12. Through which part of their body do dogs sweat?

A11. Laika

 ANSWERS

A12. Feet

Q13. Which dog breed is born pink but turns blue-back in 8 to 10 weeks?

 QUESTIONS

Q14. What type of dog breed holds the record for the longest ears?

A13. Chow Chow

 ANSWERS

A14. Tigger

Q15. In which city have stray dogs learned to ride the subway?

 QUESTIONS

Q16. Which dog breed actually cannot bark?

A15. Moscow

 ANSWERS

A16. Basenji

Q17. How many times stronger is a dog's sense of smell than that of a human's?

 QUESTIONS

Q18. Dogs can be trained to detect which serious disease in humans?

A17. 10,000 times

 ANSWERS

A18. Cancer

Q19. How many of the 12 dogs on board the Titanic survived?

 QUESTIONS

Q20. Which country has the highest dog population in the world?

A19. 3

 ANSWERS

A20. United States

Q21. What was the name of the first dog to become a Hollywood celebrity?

QUESTIONS

Q22. What is the name of Tin Tin's dog?

A21. Rin Tin Tin

 ANSWERS

A22. Snow White

Q23. What is the top health problem among dogs today?

 QUESTIONS

Q24. Which US President's pet dog ripped the pants off a visiting ambassador?

A23. Obesity

 ANSWERS

A24. Theodore Roosevelt

Q25. For how many weeks do pregnant female dogs carry their puppies in the womb?

 QUESTIONS

Q26. How many people in the US die from dog bites every year?

A25. Nine weeks

 ANSWERS

A26. 15

Q27. How many times does the Bible mention dogs?

 QUESTIONS

Q28. How many dogs in the US have been named as primary beneficiary in their owner's will?

A27. 14 times

 ANSWERS

A28. 1 million dogs

Q29. For how long have human beings kept dogs as pets?

 QUESTIONS

Q30. How many breeds of purebred dogs are there?

A29. 12,000 years

 ANSWERS

A30. 703

Q31. What is President Obama's pet dog called?

 QUESTIONS

Q32. Which dog is the national dog of France?

A31. Bo

 ANSWERS

A32. Poodle

Q33. What dog breed is Snoopy?

 ## QUESTIONS

Q34. What was the name of the dog who along with his owner won Britain's Got Talent 2015?

A33. Beagle

 ANSWERS

A34. Matisse

Q35. What dog breed is Scooby-Doo?

 QUESTIONS

Q36. Which country has a state named Chihuahua?

A35. Great Dane

 ANSWERS

A36. Mexico

Q37. Which dog breed is a playing piece in the board game Monopoly?

 QUESTIONS

Q38. Which dog breed is known as the "poor man's racehorse"?

A37. Scottish Terrier

 ANSWERS

A38. Whippet

Q39. Which dog breed was very well liked by Queen Elizabeth II?

 ## QUESTIONS

Q40. What is the name of the dog that sometimes appears in Tom and Jerry cartoons?

A39. Welsh Corgis

 ANSWERS

A40. Spike

Q41. Which dog breed has defects in kidney and liver from birth making it vulnerable to gout?

 QUESTIONS

Q42. In which country it is against the law to own a dog as a pet unless it's a guard or hunting dog?

A41. Dalmatian

 ANSWERS

A42. Iran

Q43. How fast can the greyhound, the fastest dog in the world, run in miles per hour?

 QUESTIONS

Q44. Which famous Mongol emperor holds the world record for the most dogs ever owned?

A43. 45 mph

 ANSWERS

A44. Kublai Khan

Q45. To many dogs someone showing them a smile or baring his teeth is an act of _____.

 QUESTIONS

Q46. Which dog breed is also known as the Chrysanthemum Dog?

A45. Aggression

 ANSWERS

A46. Shih Tzu

Q47. What is the ridge between the shoulders of a dog known as?

 QUESTIONS

Q48. What is a dog in a wild state generally known as?

A47. Withers

 ANSWERS

A48. Feral

Q49. Dew, mops, and splay are all related to which part of a dog?

 QUESTIONS

Q50. How long does it take for the skeletons of giant dog breeds to fully mature?

A49. Feet

 ANSWERS

A50. 2 years

Q51. How long does it take for the skeletons of toy dog breeds to fully mature?

 QUESTIONS

Q52. How many muscles does a dog have in its body?

A51. 6 months

 ANSWERS

A52. 700 muscles

Q53. Two third of a dog's body weight is carried on their ____ legs.

 QUESTIONS

Q54. What is the name of the bone between the hip and the knee in a dog?

A53. Front

 ANSWERS

A54. Femur

Q55. What is another word used to describe a dog's ankle that is also commonly used for horses?

 QUESTIONS

Q56. Over exercise as a puppy may lead to problems with the ___ when grown up.

A55. Hock

 ANSWERS

A56. Hip

Q57. The tail of a dog is an extension of which bone?

 QUESTIONS

Q58. The muscles and nerves found in the tail of a dog contribute to what digestive function?

A57. The spine

 ANSWERS

A58. Bowel control

Q59. What part of the dog's body do the words Gay, Saber, and Screw refer to?

 QUESTIONS

Q60. What is the same identifying feature of a dog as finger prints are for humans?

A59. Tail

 ANSWERS

A60. Nose print

Q61. In a Schutzhund competition dogs attack ___ people.

 QUESTIONS

Q62. When was the most recent Chinese year of the dog?

A61. Padded

 ANSWERS

A62. 2018

Q63. How many smelling cells does an Alsatian have?

 QUESTIONS

Q64. What is The African Wild Dog also known as?

A63. 220 million

 ANSWERS

A64. The Painted Wolf

Q65. George Lucas' pet dog inspired the creation of which Star Wars character?

 QUESTIONS

Q66. What are dogs a domesticated form of?

A65. Chewbaca

 ANSWERS

A66. Wolf

Q67. What are the four oval shaped pads in a dog's paw known as?

 QUESTIONS

Q68. What is the large pad in the middle of a dog's front paw known as?

A67. Digit pads

 ANSWERS

A68. Metacarpal pad

Q69. How many canine teeth does a dog have when fully grown?

 QUESTIONS

Q70. At around what age do puppy's teeth fall out to give way to adult teeth?

A69. 4

 ANSWERS

A70. 3 months

Q71. What is the hardest substance in a dog's body?

 QUESTIONS

Q72. Female dogs are generally bigger or smaller than male dogs?

A71. Enamel

 ANSWERS

A72. Smaller

Q73. Sterilisation of male dogs is known as what?

 QUESTIONS

Q74. Sterilisation of female dogs is known as what?

A73. Neutering

 ANSWERS

A74. Spaying

Q75. Although greyhounds have a reputation of being speed freaks, they are actually incredibly ___.

 QUESTIONS

Q76. Some dogs are able to understand basic ___ language.

A75. Lazy

 ANSWERS

A76. Sign

Q77. How many more times is a dog likely to bite someone or be aggressive when walked by a male?

 QUESTIONS

Q78. Which gender of dogs prefer to play with dogs of the opposite sex when young?

A77. 4 times

 ANSWERS

A78. Male dogs

Q79. Doing which activity with your dog can generally lead to better behaviour for them?

 QUESTIONS

Q80. MRI testing has shown that a canine brain can react similarly to sounds of pain as a _____ brain.

A79. Walking them

 ANSWERS

A80. Human

Q81. What is the terminology used to describe training a dog by rewarding him for good behaviour?

 QUESTIONS

Q82. What dog breed is also known as the Bernese Moutain Poo?

A81. Positive reinforcement

 ANSWERS

A82. Bernoodle

Q83. What dog breed was created in medieval France to hunt deer and boar?

 QUESTIONS

Q84. What dog breed is routinely used for search and rescue missions?

A83. Bloodhound

 ANSWERS

A84. German Shepherd

Q85. What dog breed was created to be the cherished companions of the imperial family of China?

 QUESTIONS

Q86. Which dog breed is famously known as the clowns of the canine world?

A85. Pekingese

 ANSWERS

A86. Pug

Q87. Which dog breed is one of the earliest to serve as police dogs and in the military?

 QUESTIONS

Q88. Which dog breed is a cross between the German Shepherd and Siberian Husky?

A87. Rottweiler

 ANSWERS

A88. Shepsky

Q89. Which dog breed is a cross between a Poodle and a Schnauzer?

 QUESTIONS

Q90. What is a dog breed that is a combination of different breeds rather than one identifiable breed?

A89. Schnoodle

 ANSWERS

A90. Mutt

Q91. What is a dog breed name that is also the word for inhabitants of an island nation?

 QUESTIONS

Q92. What is a dog breed name that also describes a type of pasta sauce?

A91. Maltese

 ANSWERS

A92. Bolognese

Q93. What is a dog breed name that is also the name for a type of military helicopter?

 QUESTIONS

Q94. Which Paul McCartney song features a high-pitched whistle from his dog?

A93. Chinook

 ANSWERS

A94. A Day in the Life

Q95. What is the word used to refer to a father of a dog litter?

 QUESTIONS

Q96. What is the word used to refer to a mother of a dog litter?

A95. Sire

 ANSWERS

A96. Dam

Q97. Dogs are sensitive to the Earth's ___ field.

 QUESTIONS

Q98. What is the word to describe the birth process of a dog?

A97. Magnetic

 ANSWERS

A98. Whelping

Q99. What is the word used to describe an adult male dog that is capable of reproduction?

 QUESTIONS

Q100. What is the Latin word for dog?

A99. A stud

 ANSWERS

A100. Canis

Made in the USA
Middletown, DE
16 July 2025